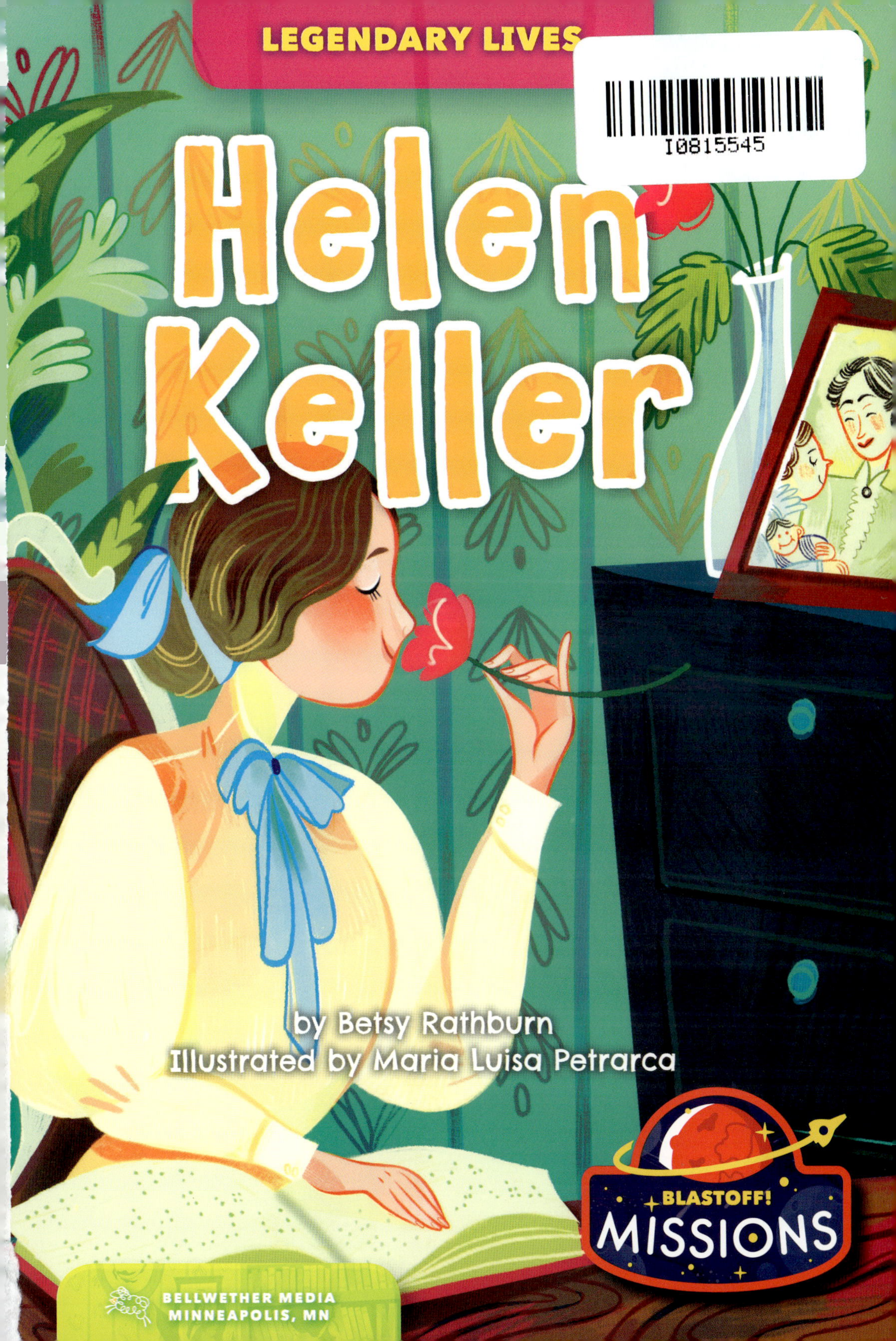
LEGENDARY LIVES
I0815545
Helen Keller
by Betsy Rathburn
Illustrated by Maria Luisa Petrarca
BLASTOFF! MISSIONS
BELLWETHER MEDIA
MINNEAPOLIS, MN

Blastoff! Missions takes you on a learning adventure! Colorful illustrations and exciting narratives highlight cool facts about our world and beyond. Read the mission goals and follow the narrative to gain knowledge, build reading skills, and have fun!

Traditional Nonfiction

Narrative Nonfiction

Blastoff! Universe

MISSION GOALS

- FIND YOUR SIGHT WORDS IN THE BOOK.
- LEARN ABOUT HELEN KELLER'S LIFE.
- LEARN HOW HELEN KELLER WORKED TO HELP PEOPLE WITH DISABILITIES.

This edition first published in 2025 by Bellwether Media, Inc.

Library of Congress Cataloging-in-Publication Data

LC record for Helen Keller available at: https://lccn.loc.gov/2024041925

Editor: Rebecca Sabelko Designer: Andrea Schneider

Printed in the United States of America, North Mankato, MN.

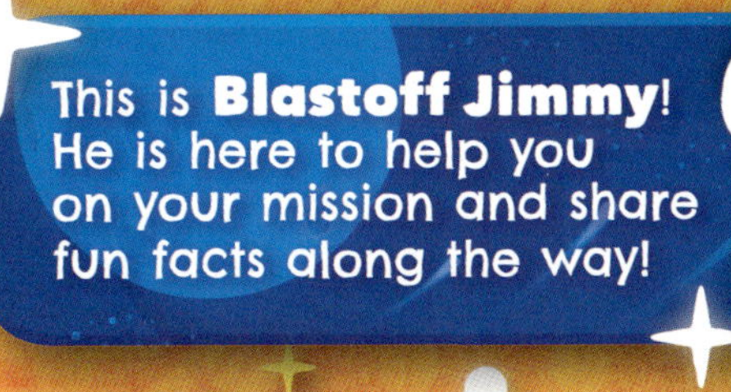

Table of Contents

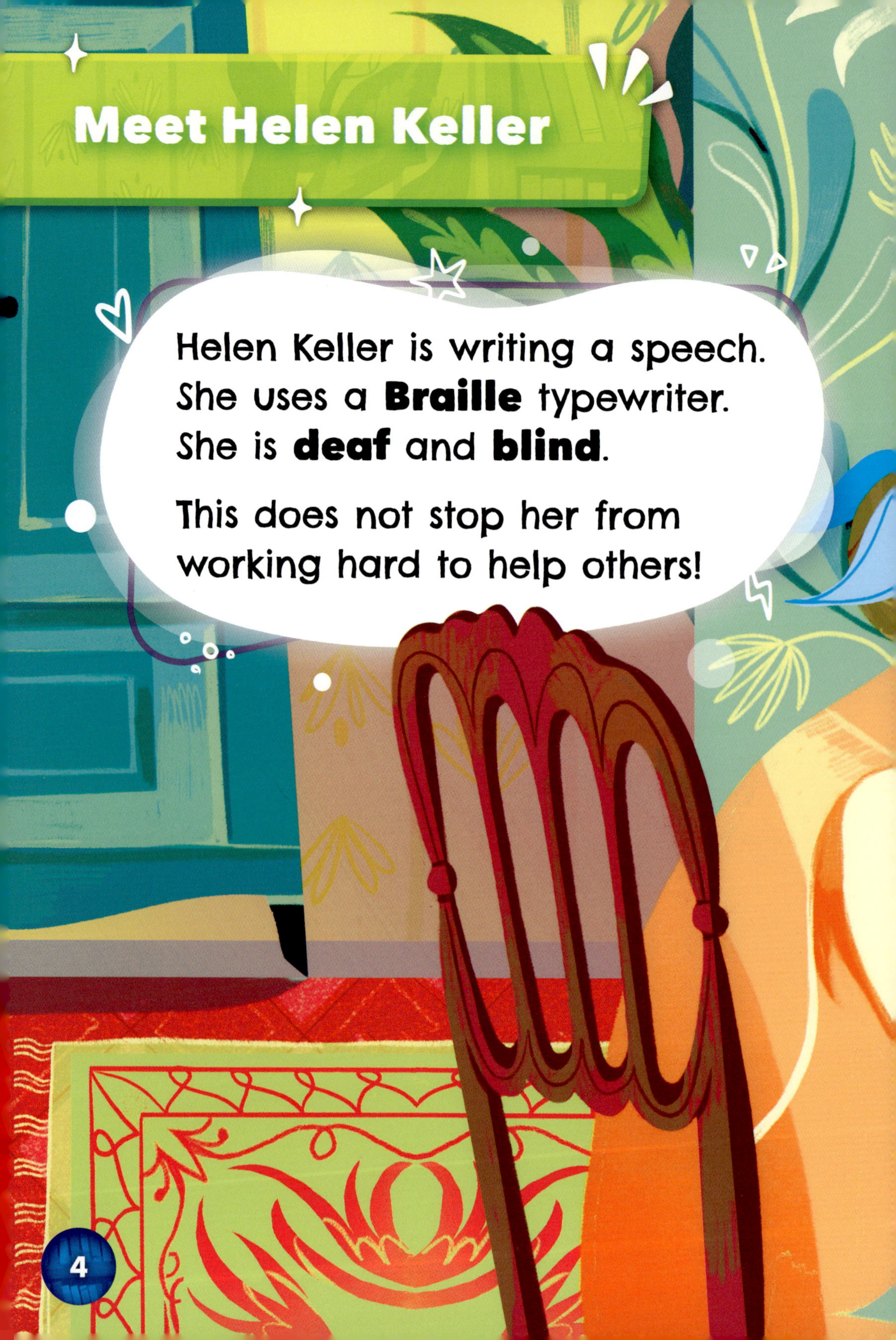

Meet Helen Keller

Helen Keller is writing a speech. She uses a **Braille** typewriter. She is **deaf** and **blind**.

This does not stop her from working hard to help others!

JIMMY SAYS
A movie was made about Helen's life in 1962. It is called *The Miracle Worker*. It won many awards!
Braille typewriter
Braille

Learning to Communicate

It is 1882. Helen is almost 2 years old. She lives in Alabama. She is very sick.

She gets better. But the sickness made her deaf and blind.

Helen has a hard time as a child. She cannot **communicate** well with her family. They seek help to teach Helen.

Anne
Sullivan

Helen is now 6. Anne Sullivan comes to stay with her family. She is Helen's teacher.

Anne works closely with Helen. She spells words on Helen's hand. Helen learns to communicate!

A Busy Life

Helen is now in school. She learns to read Braille. She also learns to speak and **lip-read**.

Her hard work pays off. She earns a **bachelor's degree** from Radcliffe College in 1904.

Now Helen is a well-known writer. She writes books. She also writes for magazines.

Many of her works are about blindness. She begins to **advocate** for people with **disabilities**.

In 1920, Helen helps create the **American Civil Liberties Union**.

She fights for the **civil rights** of all Americans!

Thank you!

Helen is in New York City. She gives a **lecture** against war.

Her lectures **inspire** many people. In 1946, she begins a **world tour**. She asks world leaders to help deaf and blind people.

Inspiring Others

It is 1964. Helen is awarded the Presidential Medal of Freedom! She wins many more honors in her life.

Helen still inspires people today. Her work helped make lives better!

Helen Keller Profile

Born

June 27, 1880,
in Tuscumbia, Alabama

Died

June 1, 1968

Accomplishments

Deaf and blind writer who worked to help people with disabilities and to fight for Americans' civil rights

Timeline

1882: Helen becomes deaf and blind after a serious sickness

1887: Anne Sullivan begins teaching Helen

1903: Helen's first book is released

1904: Helen graduates from Radcliffe College

1920: Helen helps start the American Civil Liberties Union

1964: Helen is awarded the Presidential Medal of Freedom

Glossary

advocate–to support or argue for a cause

American Civil Liberties Union–a group that fights for and protects the rights of Americans

bachelor's degree–a degree earned after four years of study at the college or university level

blind–unable to see

Braille–a system of writing that uses raised dots that people can feel to read

civil rights–the rights all people have to freedom and equal treatment under the law

communicate–to share information and feelings

deaf–unable to hear

disabilities–conditions that make it difficult for people to do certain things

inspire–to give someone an idea about what to do or create

lecture–a talk given before an audience or class

lip-read–to understand what people are saying by feeling their mouths move as they speak

world tour–a trip to different places around the world

To Learn More

AT THE LIBRARY

Bassier, Emma. *Louis Braille*. Minneapolis, Minn.: Pop!, 2020.

Pincus, Meeg. *So Much More to Helen!: The Passions and Pursuits of Helen Keller*. Ann Arbor, Mich.: Sleeping Bear Press, 2022.

Romero, Libby. *Helen Keller*. New York, N.Y.: DK Publishing, 2019.

ON THE WEB

FACTSURFER

Factsurfer.com gives you a safe, fun way to find more information.

1. Go to www.factsurfer.com.
2. Enter "Helen Keller" into the search box and click 🔍.
3. Select your book cover to see a list of related content.

BEYOND THE MISSION

> WHAT FACT FROM THE BOOK DID YOU THINK WAS THE MOST INTERESTING?

> THINK ABOUT A PERSON WHO INSPIRES YOU. WHAT DO THEY INSPIRE YOU TO ACHIEVE?

> WHAT DO YOU HOPE TO INSPIRE OTHER PEOPLE TO DO?

Index